POLITE MOMENTS

Gary & Cathy Maldaner

Psalm 27:11
Plain Path Publishers
Columbus, North Carolina

Chapter 1 – Polite Moments Volume 1   Copyright © 1991 by Gary Maldaner
Chapter 2 – Polite Moments Volume 2   Copyright © 1995 by Gary Maldaner
Chapter 3 – Polite Moments Volume 3   Copyright © 1997 by Gary Maldaner
Chapter 4 – Polite Moments Volume 4   Copyright © 1998 by Gary Maldaner
Chapter 5 – Polite Moments Volume 5   Copyright © 1998 by Gary Maldaner

All rights reserved. No part of this book may be reproduced, stored in a retrieval system, or transmitted in any form or by any means– electronic, mechanical, photocopying, recording, or otherwise without the prior written permission of the publisher, except for brief quotations in printed reviews.

All Scripture is taken from the King James Version of the Bible.

ISBN   0-9764108-0-X

Published by Plain Path Publishers
P.O. Box 830
Columbus, NC 28722

www.plainpath.org

Table of Contents

Chapter 5 – Learn to Do These Things! 95

POLITE MOMENTS

Chapter 1

General Topics

Train Yourself to Eat
Things That You Don't Like

But I keep under my body, and bring it into subjection… Your body must be trained to do things that it does not like to do so that you will be useful to the Lord as you grow up. Luke 9:23 Much of this training can take place through food. It is good for your future that you deny yourself and eat things that do not please you. Also, eating what you do not like keeps you from offending the person who has prepared the food. 1 Cor. 8:13 With a good attitude, teach yourself to eat many different kinds of foods! Accept without complaint foods that are cooked differently, not cooked, or foods that you have not tried before. John the Baptist, a man strong of character and greatly used by God, was content to eat locusts and wild honey! Mark 1:6

And seek not ye what ye shall eat, or what ye shall drink, neither be ye of doubtful mind. For all these things do the nations of the world seek after: and your Father knoweth that ye have need of these things. Luke 12:29,30

Always Be Thankful

First of all, be thankful to the Lord for the free gift of Salvation that He provided for you by shedding His blood on the cross. Rom. 5:8 Heb. 9:22 A person who is thankful for his Salvation will also be thankful for the many things that God does for him during each day. Ps. 68:18 Speak your thankfulness to anyone who does something for you; holding doors, giving you change at the store, bringing things to you, picking something up for you, cooking and washing clothes for you, giving you advice and correction, teaching you, etc. Always write thank-you notes to those who give you gifts or to those who do something special for you. Let others know that you are grateful for anything that is done for you or given to you!

In everything give thanks: for this is the
will of God in Christ Jesus concerning you.
1 Thessalonians 5:18

Always Use People's Names

People like to hear their own names! It is polite to use a person's name when you are talking to him. "Hi, John." "Good morning, Mr. Smith!" Always use the proper title with a name when talking to or about an adult outside of your family. When you are with those your own age, never call a person by his last name; this is appropriate only when necessary in sports. Always consider those to whom you are talking to be better than yourself. Phil. 2:3 Remembering and using a person's name pleases him. You are not to please others by compromising and giving in to sin, but in the position of a servant, you should seek to please others with your politeness. Using another person's name (along with a proper tone of voice) shows to him that you think that he is worthy of your respect. "Greet the friends by name." 3 Jn. 14b

Even as I please all men in all things,
not seeking mine own profit, but the profit
of many, that they might be saved.
1 Corinthians 10:33

Do Not Cause Fear to an Older or Weaker Person

You will offend others when you cause them to be fearful. Offending others hurts your testimony. Prov. 22:1 The after-church snowball fight or game of tag may have to be postponed – if others may worry about being hurt. Take special care when playing, running, or riding your bike around older persons, those who have physical disabilities, or young children. Do not cause undue fear when playing ball or using weapons (guns, bow and arrow, etc.) near others' houses. Be cautious with motorized equipment, and respect others' property and belongings. When visiting at other houses (friends, grandparents, etc.), be especially careful – what you are allowed to do at your house may not be acceptable to other adults.

That ye may approve things that are excellent;
that ye may be sincere and without offense
till the day of Christ. Philippians 1:10

Do Nothing to Draw Attention to Yourself

It is not the purpose of your face and body to be used to get attention for yourself. Attention drawn to yourself is gain for you – and loss for Christ. Phil. 3:7 Your body is to "magnify" Jesus Christ. As others look at you, and see the way that you live (your speech, behavior, and attitudes), they should think more of Jesus Christ. Phil. 1:20 John 3:30 Rom. 6:19,20 When you show off, Jesus Christ is not magnified, honored, or glorified. 1 Cor. 10:31 The more you try to exalt yourself, the less use you will be to the Lord. 2 Cor. 12:7-10 Let others say good things about you; consider yourself to be an "unprofitable servant." Prov. 27:2 Luke 17:10 Those who use their faces, voices, and bodies to draw attention to themselves are conforming to the world. Rom. 12:1,2

For if a man think himself to be something, when
he is nothing, he deceiveth himself. Galatians 6:3

Always Be Clean and Neat

Worldly young people of each generation, as they grow up, have the attitude of, "Let us make a name." Gen. 11:4 Each new generation wants to make its impression on the world by its resistance to the old traditions. "Look at us, and give us the recognition that we deserve!" Today's generation has chosen the messy, sloppy, lack-of-character look. Christians should therefore make an effort to be different, rather than to copy the world so as to gain favor from the people of the world. Gal. 1:10 Jer. 2:33

Choose a hairstyle that looks as if you have made an effort to keep your hair orderly – not a tangled mess or a proud, spiked look. Clothes should be those that do not draw attention to yourself; and should be clean, ironed, and properly tucked and buttoned – avoiding the loose, "I'm available" appearance. Shoes should be tied, belts should be worn with clothes that have belt loops, and colors should be matched and sex-appropriate. When in public, avoid wearing clothes that are too tight, over-sized, or improper for the situation. Zeph. 1:8

Be clean and neat in your habits. Avoid borrowing personal items, and avoid being offensive through an unwashed face, dirty fingernails, or bad habits (such as chewing your nails in public). Learn and practice proper table manners at home so that you are prepared to make a good impression when you eat away from home.

Therefore, brethren, stand fast, and hold the traditions which ye have been taught, whether by word, or our epistle.
2 Thessalonians 2:15

Go out of Your Way to Find Ways to Help Others

Become to others what they need, for the cause of Jesus Christ. Always have the attitude of, "What can I do to help this person?" "How could the Lord use me in this person's life?" Be eager and willing to comfort someone, carry groceries, open doors, rake leaves, shovel snow, wash windows, etc. Have no thought of receiving gain for yourself – whether in money or praise. Try to put yourself in another's place, and unselfishly give of yourself. Phil. 2:4 Be willing to show the love of Jesus Christ to others, and then be faithful in sharing the Gospel with them through words or with a tract. Mark 16:15,16

For though I be free from all men, yet have I made myself servant unto all, that I might gain the more. To the weak became I as weak, that I might gain the weak: I am made all things to all men, that I might by all means save some. 1 Corinthians 9:19,22

Give Your Mother Flowers

Make a special effort to please your parents, who have given you your family and your home. Go beyond submissive obedience in showing love to them, and think of ways to cause them to be joyful! A young person who is thoughtful of his parents will do the unexpected to please them. Give your mother flowers (your father his slippers), offer to do the dishes, wash the car, or volunteer to do some other chore that is not normally your job. Write notes to your parents, make things for them, and buy gifts for them at any time during the year. Be willing to give of yourself to spend time with your parents. Be loving, patient, encouraging, understanding, and thankful. When you are away from home, remember that what others think of you is often what they think of your parents. Are you polite, well-mannered, thoughtful, and well-behaved? Do you live a life that is pleasing to your parents when you are away from them?

The proverbs of Solomon. A wise son maketh a glad father: but a foolish son is the heaviness of his mother. The glory of children are their fathers. Proverbs 10:1; 17:6b

Show Strong Character
to the Outside World

Let the world easily recognize you as a Christian! Since *man looketh on the outward appearance*, (1 Sam. 16:7) nothing identifies you as quickly as does your clothing, hairstyle, facial expressions, body movements, speech, and interests. When you are out in public, be neatly and modestly dressed – without following the styles of the world. Deut. 22:5 Stand up straight, sit up straight, and walk with a determination that shows that there is something different about you. Have a pleasant expression on your face, and let the tone of your voice show that you are submissive to Divine authority. Pronounce your words carefully, making sure that your speech is dependable and sensible. Titus 2:8 Prov. 21:23; 29:11 Do not speak foolishly. Keep away from impure speech, books, and magazines. Ep. 5:4 2 Tim. 2:23 Be eager to help, and be a hard worker! Be a joyful person to be around, and keep yourself from being offended by the rudeness of the world. Ps. 16:11; 119:165

But ye are a chosen generation, a royal priesthood,
an holy nation, a peculiar people; that ye should show
forth the praises of him who hath called you out of
darkness into his marvelous light. 1 Peter 2:9

Look at People When You Are Talking With Them

The face is a reflection of your inner thoughts, and your eyes are described in the Bible as the *light of the body*. Mt. 6:22 It is polite to allow a person who is talking to you to see your face and eyes. There is much more to communication than words. The expressions on your face show interest, eagerness, concern, tenderness, friendliness, and many other feelings from within yourself. The eyes and facial expressions can also reveal selfishness, pride, rebellion, deceitfulness, greed, and hardness of heart. Prov. 23:6,7; 28:22; 30:13 Is. 3:9 Jer. 5:3 When talking with another person of any age, look politely into his eyes; do not stare or look away for too long. When you are being corrected by someone, look at him with respect; your facial expression helps him to know how to talk to you.

As in water face answereth to
face, so the heart of man to man.
Proverbs 27:19

Always Stand and Meet the Company

Make an effort to come and greet those who have come to visit your family. Be friendly, but do not try to draw attention to yourself. Put down or stop what you are doing, look at the visitors, and shake hands firmly. After you have met the visitors, allow the adults to talk together without interruption. If you are welcomed to stay with the adults, listen quietly unless you are encouraged to take part in the conversation. If there are children that you can take care of or play with, be sure that your activities do not disturb the conversations of the adults. Make sure that in all that you do when company comes to your house you are helping to build up the reputation of your family.

A good name is rather to be chosen
than great riches, and loving favour rather
than silver and gold.   Proverbs 22:1

Never Interrupt

Unless there is an emergency, it is impolite to interrupt other people when they are talking to someone, watching something, or doing a job. Respectfully wait until a conversation is over before talking to someone. When walking between two people who are talking together or in front of people who are watching something, always say, "Excuse me." When someone is doing a job, politely wait until you are recognized before distracting him. If a person is writing or reading, wait until he completes a portion of his work and looks at you. When with a friend, be careful that your conversation or activities do not interrupt the conversations or activities of others. If you are being taught by someone, do not start to do something else before he is finished talking to you. Always think, "How would I like to be treated by others?"

Let nothing be done through strife or vainglory;
but in lowliness of mind let each esteem
other better than themselves. Philippians 2:3

How to Behave
in the House of God

Although God no longer lives within the church building (He lives within the body of each Christian – 1 Cor. 6:19,20), the place where you go to worship God is still a special place. The church is a place where you should be on your best behavior – showing an honor and reverence for a building that is called "God's house." The church is also a place to meet and fellowship with friends, but not a place to gossip, make fun of others, or act silly and foolish. The best place to sit is with your family, but if you are permitted and choose to sit with friends, sit in a place where you will not be tempted to talk during the service. Young people who "migrate" to the back of the church (as far away from the preacher and their parents as they can get) are likely to distract others and not pay attention. Leave the back rows open for those who may have to arrive late to church.

Unless you have an emergency, do not leave to get a drink or go to the restroom during the service. Sneeze or blow your nose in such a way as to not draw attention to yourself. Keep your eyes on what is going on in front of the church; avoid watching or talking to others, reading, or looking out of the windows. Do not damage God's house by putting your feet on the pew, by leaving trash, or by folding back the cover of the songbook. Take an active part in the service by

singing as well as you can and by looking up verses as they are used by your pastor. Do nothing that might distract other people who are listening to the service, but rather set a good example for others (especially younger children) to look to.

At the end of the service, respond to the invitation if you need to (not because of what someone else does or doesn't do) or quietly pray for others. Do not use this time to put your coat on and prepare to leave.

The clothing that you wear to church should be modest, neat, and clean. Unless for some reason you cannot change before coming to church, avoid coming to God's house dressed in athletic or work clothes.

That thou mayest know how thou oughtest
to behave thyself in the house of God, which
is the church of the living God, the pillar
and ground of the truth. 1 Timothy 3:15

Be on Time

The way that you talk about time and the way that you live by time openly shows to others much about your character. Commit yourself to words, and then make sure that your behavior shows that your words are trustworthy and dependable. Deut. 23:23a When you say, "I will be there by eight o'clock," then make sure that you arrive before (but not too far ahead of time) or at eight o'clock. Make sure that you arrive on time when you return home, make phone calls when you say that you will, complete assignments on time, complete your chores on time (without being reminded), and answer letters promptly. When working for others, arrive at your job early enough to receive instruction, and then work until the assigned time is over. Arriving late, taking longer breaks than allowed, or leaving early are all ways of stealing from your employer. When you need to have others do things for you (washing clothes, taking you somewhere, fixing a special meal, etc.), ask far enough ahead of time to give them a chance to help you in addition to taking care of their own responsibilities.

That which is gone out of thy lips thou shalt
keep and perform. Deuteronomy 23:23a

Listen, and Show An Interest In Other People

A Christian young person should be "swift to hear, slow to speak." James 1:19 Train yourself to be an eager, attentive listener. Do not listen only for the purpose of waiting to say something about yourself or your own interests. Show an interest in others and their topics of conversation. Ask questions to show your interest as well as to learn more. Practice with others by having conversations in which you listen and ask questions about the topic being discussed, and talk about yourself only when asked something by the other person. The person who listens and shows an interest in others is the one who is usually able to direct the conversation by asking more questions. Your goal in any conversation with an unsaved person should be to talk to him about Jesus Christ. Show a concern for others, giving up your own interests, and always being ready to help another person with your words.

But sanctify the Lord God in your hearts: and be ready always to give an answer to every man that asketh you a reason of the hope that is in you with meekness and fear. 1 Peter 3:15

18

Always Be Obedient

It is polite to be obedient because obedience shows a respect for a person who has been placed over you by God. Your tone of voice and facial expression should show that you are willing to submit to the desire of the person who has asked you to do something. Heb. 13:17 Disobedience shows to your teacher or parent that you think that what you want to do is more important than what he has asked you to do. Prov. 14:12 When you disobey, you put yourself in the place of authority, and your Mom or Dad becomes the one who is to change and obey you by allowing you to have your own way. Obey your parents (or whoever they have asked to be in charge of you) whether they are watching you or not, and obey them as a way of pleasing the Lord. Col. 3:22-24

Your obedience should not depend upon how you are treated. Answer politely and be kind toward those who treat you unkindly. 1 Peter 2:18-20 Always remember that being obedient and submissive to those in authority over you is a way of showing your love to God. John 14:23

Children, obey your parents in the Lord: for this is right. Honour thy father and mother; which is the first commandment with promise; that it may be well with thee, and thou mayest live long on the earth. Ephesians 6:1-3

Learn Through Respectful Questioning

Seek wisdom and understanding by often asking your parents serious questions. Learn as much as you can about how to live as a Christian, how to be a husband or wife, how to be a parent, and how to seek God's will for your own life. Listen to instruction as if your life depended upon it – it does! Prov. 1:5; 4:17 In planning your life, "lean not unto thine own understanding," and "be not wise in thine own eyes." Prov. 3:5,6 Never be proud by thinking that you know more than your parents. Be honest and open with your parents in asking for their counsel about your friendships, your work, the growth of your body, right and wrong, and the circumstances of daily life. Prov. 15:22 If necessary, ask your parents for a time alone when you can talk with them.

Ask questions politely! Make sure that your questions are not deceitful, foolish, disrespectful, or meant to challenge authority. 2 Tim. 2:23 Never seek to find out details about sinful practices. Rom. 16:19

Happy is the man that findeth wisdom,
and the man that getteth understanding.
Proverbs 3:13

Befriend Those
Who Are Unsaved

Your greatest goal in life is to serve the Lord by reaching others for Jesus Christ. Mt. 28:19,20   Until you become an adult, you should be friendly to adult strangers only when you are with your parents or another familiar adult. You can practice your friendliness to strangers by being friendly and concerned toward those your own age or younger.   Remember that your friendliness toward any unsaved person is only for the purpose of leading him to Jesus Christ. Be unafraid as you seek to witness for your Savior. Jer. 1:5-8 Learn how to start a conversation by asking questions and directing the topic of conversation toward spiritual things. Begin with general questions ("What do you like to do?") and then direct the conversation toward the spiritual ("Where do you go to church?" "Do you know that you are going to Heaven when you die?"). Use every opportunity to witness for Jesus Christ!

For I was an hungered, and ye gave me meat:
I was thirsty, and ye gave me drink; I was a stranger,
and ye took me in: naked, and ye clothed me: I was
in prison, and ye came unto me. Matthew 25:35,36

Use Your Time Wisely

Take the time to do the things that you are responsible for doing! You are a steward of the time that God gives to you each day, and you should not misuse this valuable gift. 1 Cor. 4:2 Ep. 5:15-17 A young person who is concerned about knowing and doing God's will each day will not have to say, "I didn't have time to do it." The Lord will give you time to do all the things that you are given to do by parents and teachers, and time to do the things that you need to do for yourself and for friends. A person who claims to not have time to do something arranges his time in the wrong way, works too slowly, or does not want to do it.

Don't waste time! Always be busy with something that will help you to become more like Jesus Christ. All that you do – play, work, thinking, sports, study, watching T.V., games, or reading should in some way bring glory to God. 1 Cor. 10:31 In doing that, you will become more like Him, because you are using the time He has given you to do what He wants you to do.

See then that ye walk circumspectly, not
as fools, but as wise, redeeming the time,
because the days are evil. Epesians 5:15,16

POLITE
MOMENTS

Chapter Two

Visiting Other Families

"Can You Come Over To My House?"

An invitation has been received from a friend or relative! First, be sure that it is a proper invitation. Have your friend's parents given permission for you to come over? Your parents may want to know this when you ask for their permission. Be ready to give more details about your visit. How long will you be gone? What time are you to arrive, and when are you to leave? What will you be doing? Will you be going somewhere else? Who else will be at your friend's house? Have you been invited for a meal? Do you have any responsibilities at home that may need to be given to someone else if you leave?

Give to your parents whatever information they ask for, and then allow them time to make a decision. Do not get upset if they show concern for you by asking for more information.

Sometimes you may want to ask for an invitation either over the phone or at your friend's house. Avoid going to another person's house without an invitation (offered or requested) just to "hang around" without his parent's consent.

Honour thy father and mother; (which is the first commandment with promise;) that it may be well with thee, and thou mayest live long on the earth.
Ephesians 6:2,3

Ask – Don't Inform!

One who is to be in submission to authority must be careful about how he speaks when seeking permission to do something or to go somewhere. Seeking permission does not include stating your intentions. "I'm going over to John's house – O.K.?" When you have already decided and stated what you plan to do, your parents are no longer given the full freedom to decide how to answer you. Ask permission without assuming or encouraging a certain answer from your parents. Always let your parents know that you are willing to accept, without complaint, the decision that they will make for you.

If your parents make the decision not to allow you to go to another person's house, do not try to change their minds by begging ("Pleeeeease!"), making promises ("If you'll let me... I will..."), bribing ("I'll... if you will let me..."), or pouting (being miserable to make your parents feel guilty). Never demand a reason ("Why not?") or argue with your parents. Phil. 2:14 Each of these behaviors show that you were not asking for permission – but were only expecting to have your parents agree with your plans.

I delight to do thy will, O my God. Psalm 40:8a

26

"Let's Play in the Yard."

Unlike pill bottles, most yards are not "child-proof." Although you or your friend may consider the yard to be your private play area, it belongs to and is cared for by adults. Adults have a different purpose for a yard than you do, although you may become a part of their purpose in having a yard.

When visiting someone else's yard, find out about his "yard rules" and also use the "yard rules" that you have learned from your own parents. Beyond knowing and obeying these yard rules, you also need to consider what might offend others who may place a high value on the condition of their yard. You may be allowed to ride your bike anywhere across your yard – other families may have such well-tended grass that the sight of a bike traveling across the lawn would bring grief to your friend's parents.

As you enter another person's yard, ask yourself: "What areas of the yard should I stay away from? What things in the yard are fragile? How does the weather affect how I use the yard?" You will become an unwelcome guest if you turn the yard into a mud pit, break the concrete flamingo, and accidentally step on the long-awaited watermelon.

Look not every man on his own things, but every man also on the things of others. Philippians 2:4
Philippians 2:4

27

"You Can Have This!"

A young friend is likely to be so happy to play with you that he may want to show you his thankfulness by giving you something. "You can have this" may mean, "You can have this until I want it back." Also, the thing that is being given to you may not be something that his parents would want him to be giving away. The thing being given may have more value to his parents than it does to the child. A child may quickly give away a $30 toy that he has little interest in at the moment. Think about the age and maturity of the child who is offering you something. Who actually owns the object? Should he be giving it away? Would your parents want you to bring it home ("You can have my pet snake.")? Why is he giving this to me? (Ex. 28:8 Prov. 17:23)

If you are unsure about receiving the gift, ask your friend's parents– preferably in private. "Jason said that I could have this. Is it all right with you that he gave it to me?" Always ask in a tone of voice that shows his parents that you are willing to accept any answer. Do not become attached to something before you are sure that it can belong to you.

If you know that you shouldn't take the thing that is offered to you or if you ask and find out that it is not to be given away, think of a way to politely refuse what you have been offered. "Thank you for offering that to me, but I would like you to keep it." Or, "I know that your parents would want you to keep this."

And let the
peace of God rule
in your hearts
Colossians 3:15a

"Who's in Charge Here?"

Every young person has within him a desire to rule – to be in charge and to make decisions that he thinks will benefit him the most. Commands from those supposedly in charge are filtered through the feelings, and anything that displeases will be challenged. "What about my rights? What about fairness? What about my ability? What about my free time? What is it going to cost me? Others can be in charge only as long as they command me to do those things that please me!"

Wherever you go, be a willing follower of those in authority and a willing follower of that which is good. 1 Thes. 5:15 Never go to someone else's home and begin to "test" those in authority to see what you can get away with. With one who is your own age, be willing to allow him to lead in activities when you are at his house. Because you are the guest, he is in the position of being "in charge," but always under the authority of his parents.

Servants, obey in all things your masters according to the flesh; not with eyeservice, as menpleasers; but in singleness of heart, fearing God. Colossians 3:22

"Is this All Right with Your Parents?"

Rules will be different when you visit at another person's house. Be alert to know what the rules are, and ask your friend or friend's parents if in doubt. What is allowed or forbidden at your house may not be the same at your friend's house. Also, never assume that other children will follow their own parents' rules – but you should.

Be willing to obey rules that you do not have at your house. If you find that there are a lack of rules needed to prevent sin or to ensure safety, follow what your own parents and the Lord would have you to do.

My son, hear the instruction of thy father, and
forsake not the law of thy mother. Proverbs 1:8

Be Friendly!

Sometimes young people act like they have "tunnel vision" and can "see" only their friends. At church you might see teenagers with blank stares navigating through a group of adults – but somehow fully coming to alertness and joy when meeting a friend.

Learn to be outgoing when visiting at other people's homes. Instead of entering the house with the attitude of, "Here I am – talk to me now," you should be willing to start the conversation. "Good morning, Mrs.___! How are you today?" Show an interest in others by being the first to speak and by asking questions that express a concern for another person. Remember those things that you are told, so that you can use this knowledge in future conversations. ("You told me last week that your aunt was in the hospital. Has she been able to come home yet?") Speak clearly, have good eye contact, and be willing to spend some time with people other than the one whom you came to visit.

When leaving the home, seek out your friend's parents to tell them that you enjoyed coming to their home and to thank them again for any special things that they did for you – providing your meals, taking you somewhere, etc.

A man that hath friends must shew
himself friendly. Proverbs 18:24a

31

Safety!

Even though you may not realize it, other parents are concerned about your safety. Great distress can be caused when you are injured on someone else's property. Knowing this, you should show to other parents that you are making an effort to be careful. In this way, they will not feel that you need to be constantly watched.

Be careful around unknown pets and around farm animals; and be cautious around machinery such as lawn mowers, tractors, or other farm equipment. Stay away from moving cars or trucks, fire, or other dangers inside or outside of the house. If necessary to assure others' parents about your concern for safety, ask permission to do things that you are unsure about – such as climbing trees. Show a concern for the safety of others by being careful with bikes, balls, bow and arrows, stones, guns, power tools, etc.

> Whoso removeth stones shall be hurt therewith; and
> he that cleaveth wood shall be endangered thereby.
> Ecclesiastes 10:9

"Please Don't Do That!"

As you receive correction and guidance from your own family, be willing to accept correction, when needed, from other adults. When visiting a friend, recognize that his parents have the rule over you and can correct you as your own parents would correct you. Answer politely when you are corrected, and immediately stop what you were doing. Other adults may not physically discipline you, but they are to "withhold not correction from the child." Prov. 23:13a

Correction may also come from your friend or from older children. You are in unfamiliar surroundings at another person's home, and may face situations or dangers that you do not know about. Always be willing to learn about the proper use of things or about proper behavior in new situations.

Open rebuke is better than secret love.
Faithful are the wounds of a friend; but
the kisses of an enemy are deceitful.
Proverbs 27:5,6

People Are
Important – Not Things!

    Your most important purpose in being with another person is for Christian fellowship. If some were honest, they would have to ask "Can I go over to Jason's house to play with his toys?" Some would befriend another only because of his things, and would be content to play with these things with or without the other person present.

    When fellowship with another person is your reason for going to someone's house, you will find just as much enjoyment in helping the other person to weed the garden as you would in playing a game.

But Martha was cumbered about much serving,
and came to him, and said, Lord, dost thou not care
that my sister hath left me to serve alone? Bid her
therefore that she help me. And Jesus answered and
said unto her, Martha, Martha, thou art careful and
troubled about many things: But one thing is needful:
and **Mary hath chosen that good part**, which
shall not be taken away from her.
Luke 10:40-42

"Can I Look at This?"

It is impolite to enter another person's house and begin to pick up, examine, or use their things. This also applies to your friend's bedroom. Another family should not feel the need to "batten down the hatches" and put anything of value or anything breakable out of sight just because you are coming over.

Taking or using things also applies to books, magazines, or letters. Do not read things on desks or tables unless you are invited to or given permission. Do not take things that you think may be of no value– unless you have permission. Even that which is in the trash can is not yours to freely take from someone else's house. Until officially discarded away from the house, the trash also belongs to someone else.

Be even more careful of other people's property than you are of your own. Think about how you would like to have others handle or play with your own things. Always have permission to look at or to play with things that are not understood to be "open to the public." Also, avoid examining the contents of the refrigerator or taking inventory of the toys and games in the closet.

And as ye would that men should do to
you, do ye also to them likewise. Luke 6:31

"I Broke It"

When visiting in another home, accidents may happen even if you are being careful. If you break something, be willing to be honest and admit to what you have done rather than avoiding the truth about what happened ("I dropped it and broke it" instead of "It fell and broke."). Sincerely offer to pay for or replace what you have broken.

Breaking something that belongs to your friend is no less important than breaking something that belongs to another member of his family. Be willing to offer restitution if you break, lose, or harm in some other way something that belongs to your friend or his family.

If fire break out, and catch in thorns, so that the stacks of corn, or the standing corn, or the field, be consumed, therewith; he that kindleth the fire shall surely make restitution. Exodus 22:6

"What Should We Talk About?"

When you visit another home, remember that every family has a private life into which you should not invade. Avoid asking questions about discipline, correction, sins of others, or other information that could easily be used as gossip. In the same way, you should not pass on private information about your parents or brothers and sisters. Prov. 11:13; 18:8 Do not get in arguments in other families. Prov. 26:17 Be careful in your talk about other people. Abstain from being critical of adults or brothers and sisters. God is not pleased when you report the sins of others and cover up your own sins and weaknesses. Prov. 11:9

Do not allow conversation that is unclean, makes fun of individuals or groups of people, or makes fun of the body – God's creation. Ep. 5:4 Sex should be discussed only with your parents or between you and a friend in the presence of a concerned, Godly adult.

Be tactful in all of your conversations. Do not blurt out without thinking. Avoid discussing sensitive topics at the wrong time (such as talking about dead animals while eating). At all times, examine your thoughts before speaking! Prov. 15:28; 12:18

Above all, always be willing to say, *"I will speak of the glorious honour of thy majesty, and of thy wondrous works."* Psalms 145:5

Set a watch,
O Lord, before my
mouth; keep the
door of my lips.
Psalm 141:3

"Come and Dine"
John 21:12

When invited to share in a meal at someone's home, be sure to follow the manners that you have been taught, and be ready to quickly learn a few more! Eating at home is usually a more casual affair compared to eating out – where you are likely to be watched by adults who will look for the results of your training at home.

Quietly accept the menu, and eat what is set before you. Do not complain, express your dislike, or make faces at the food. At home, you might "dig in" with no hesitation, but when you are a guest, wait until your host is seated and has started eating before you start. If you are unsure about how to eat a particular food, follow the example of the adults who are present. You may be used to picking up pieces of chicken, but if the adults use a knife and fork, follow their example. Do not discuss what you have to eat at your house. Take second helpings (if desired) only if offered, and eat at a pace similar to that of others at the table. Express your thankfulness for the meal after you have eaten and before you go home.

Never be ashamed to pray before you eat – even if this is not done by others around you. Quietly bow your head to express your thankfulness to the One Who supplies all things!

Not that I speak in respect of want: for I have learned,
in whatsoever state I am, therewith to be content.
Philippians 4:11

"Can I Help?"

A parasite is a creature who always takes things away from another creature and never gives anything or does anything for the one who is sacrificing its life for him. Many young people act like parasites– always ready and willing to be fed, taken places, clothed, spoken to, and otherwise pleased in some way.

Your friend may have jobs to do around the house – be willing to help instead of thinking that you came only to be entertained. Be willing to help his parents with dishes, cleaning, yard work, etc. When you visit another family, remember that their family does not stop their normal family life because you have arrived. It is much easier for a family to have a guest who is willing to fit in and is eager to help with any work that needs to be done – especially on longer visits or overnight visits.

As we have therefore opportunity, let us do
good unto all men, especially unto them who are
of the household of faith. Galatians 6:10

The Overnight Visit

There may be an occasion when you stay overnight at another person's house, by permission or by necessity. Be sure to be well prepared with those things that you need for personal care – clean clothes, personal grooming supplies, and any special medicines. Instead of "moving in" as if the house belongs to you, enter the house seeking the will of your host. "Where should I put my....?" "Which towel should I use?" "When should I....?" "What time should I be ready for breakfast?" Be prepared to have a different schedule than you do at your house, and be ready to give up certain "luxuries" that you may be used to having. Be sure not to act as if you expect certain things, and try to keep from being a burden to those who are allowing you to stay with their family.

You should not give up some things when at another person's house. If you have a habit of having personal devotions and prayer at night, try to find a time and place where you can continue to do this. Even though your parents may not be present to "prompt" you, remember to brush your teeth, to wash your face, and to do other personal things that help you to be "presentable."

Clothes that you choose should be appropriate for planned activities, and clothes that identify you as a "new creature in Christ." 1 Thes. 5:17 Be clean, modest, and neat whether you plan to play in the house, go for a hike, or retire to bed.

This is a faithful saying, and these things I will that thou affirm constantly, that they which have believed in God might be careful to maintain good works. Titus 3:8a

"Thank You Very Much!"

Today's generation is often unthankful. 2 Timothy 3:2 Many young people consider only their own special needs or desires and act as if other people exist only to willingly provide for their every wish. A Christian is to demand nothing and should be thankful for all that comes into his life!

Your thankfulness is to be directed toward the Lord and toward people – not necessarily toward things. You may not enjoy some things that are given to you (such as correction, discipline, foods that you don't like, clothes that don't fit, etc.). Enjoyable or not, be thankful that another person has taken the time, effort, thought, or money to give something to you for your enjoyment or for your good.

In every thing give thanks: for this is the
will of God in Christ Jesus concerning you.
1 Thessalonians 5:18

41

"I Have to Go Now"

When and how do you leave from another person's house? If you have a definite time that you must be home, be careful to watch the time and leave early enough so that you can arrive home on time. If you have no definite time to leave, then you must make your own wise decision.

There are other reasons why you might shorten your visit. Perhaps your friend's family is preparing a meal for which you have not been invited. Perhaps they are preparing to depart or to engage in some family activity that does not appear to include you. Your host may politely ask you to stay for a meal while secretly hoping that you will decide to leave. You must learn to determine when your welcome is expiring by seeking verbal or non-verbal "clues."

Sometimes you may have to leave another person's home because of some activity that is to take place that you are not allowed to do (by your parents) or choose not to do because you believe it is wrong. This may be a video or T.V. program, a certain type of game, or an activity that you do not take part in. Be polite in excusing yourself from these things; be unoffensive, but also honest if asked for a reason. Be willing to say, "I can't do that because I'm a Christian," and be ready to politely explain your reason. 1 Peter 3:15

If your parents are to come and get you, be ready ahead of time. Do not make them wait for you! If your parents are already at the house where you have been, stop playing when they tell you that it is time to go – even if they continue to talk with the adults. Excuses never justify disobedience!

Withdraw thy foot
from thy neighbour's
house; lest he be
weary of thee,
and so hate thee.
Proverbs 25:17

Home Again!

Come home on time, with a good report, and with having been a good representative for your family. Come home and fit quickly and quietly back into your family, rather than coming home discontented because you have been comparing your family with another. It should make no difference to you that another person gets to eat whatever he wants, gets to play more than you do, and seems to have a much "better" life than you do. Remember that when you visit other people's families, they may make the attempt to present their family as other than it really is when you are not around. 2 Cor. 10:12

Always recognize that your family is the best family that you could have, because it is the family that God, in his wisdom, has given to you! Phil. 3:13

Better is the sight of the eyes
than the wandering of the desire.
Ecclesiastes 6:9a

"What a Polite Young Person He Is!"

What is being said or thought about you as you depart from a visit to another family's home? Do they breathe a sigh of relief and wonder if you have ever had any training from your parents? Do they hope that their son or daughter will find a more polite and thoughtful friend? Do you hope that your parents will not ask about your behavior?

Are you a welcome guest in other people's homes? Do other parents cringe and hesitate when asked if you could come over to their house? Are you considered by others to be an obedient, Godly young person?

Because of the way that you act, what do other adults think about the rest of your family? When you leave your family to go to another person's home, you are a representative of your family. Adults judge a family by its products – the children. When with another family, remember that you are the guest. Do not enter another family and expect to do all of those things that you do at home. Yield your will to the desires of those whom you are visiting. Be polite and considerate of others. Guard your reputation as if it were a valuable treasure! Seek to grow each day *in favour with man*. Luke 2:52 Show a desire to please by prompt obedience, asking permission ("Is it all right if I..."), and seeking to know unspoken wishes ("Should I take my shoes off before I come in?").

A good name is rather to be chosen than great riches, and loving favour rather than silver and gold. Proverbs 22:1

"Let's Go Visit Aunt Sue!"

Aunt Sue – the one who watches while you "enjoy" her asparagus pie, the one who always wants to describe her latest operation, and the one who always pinches your cheek and says, "My, how you have grown!" How should you act when you are asked to visit your more distant relatives or friends of your parents? Keep in mind the admonition to *in lowliness of mind let each esteem other better than themselves.* Phil. 2:3

Be determined to be a blessing to someone else instead of expecting others to be a blessing to you (by satisfying your desires for food, conversation, and entertainment). Willingly go with your parents on visits that they make to other adults. Plan ahead to enjoy a visit that you know will not please your selfish nature. Be ready, with contentment and a pleasant attitude, to discuss what you might consider "uninteresting" topics, to eat what you would consider to be disagreeable food, or to do nothing but be friendly and sociable.

He that hath no rule over his own
spirit is like a city that is broken down,
and without walls. Proverbs 25:28

The Phone Visit

When you talk to someone on the phone, you are, in a way, entering into his home and into his family life. Be polite on the phone ("May I please speak to....?") and be aware of the amount of time that you spend talking to your friend. Phone conversations should usually be brief and should be made at convenient times. Be sensitive to other considerations such as long distance charges, calling a home where the phone is also used in a business, or large families where personal phone use is limited.

As you would ask to visit in person, it is also polite to ask your parents if you can use the phone – also telling them who it is that you desire to call. During this "phone visit" do not be foolish, secretive, or in other ways cause your parents to regret giving you permission for this visit. As should be true of a visit in person, a phone visit should in some way bring glory to God!

Whether therefore ye eat, or drink, or whatsoever
ye do, do all to the glory of God. 1 Corinthians 10:31

POLITE
MOMENTS

Chapter 3
Working for Others

Looking Ahead

Most of your job training comes long before you ever accept your first job outside of your family. When the time comes for you to seek this kind of job, you should be able to list your qualifications – even though you have no prior job history. Your qualifications include the attitude that you have toward work and authority, the work skills that you have learned, and the responsibility that you show in your life.

Before looking for a job, learn how to, with a good attitude, serve submissively under authority. Learn to do neat, careful work. Learn to keep your mind on your work and to work well despite distractions. Ask questions and learn how to do as many things as you can. Different types of work experience and knowledge will be useful to you in the future. Prov. 27:23 Learn to work without complaining or stopping when you get tired. Phil. 2:14,15 Learn to be a diligent worker! 2 Thes. 3:10

Work is important to the Lord. To *present your bodies a living sacrifice* to Him means that you give your life to serve Him through whatever work he would desire for you to do, paid or unpaid. This is *your reasonable service*. Rom 12:1

Prepare thy work without, and make It fit for
thyself in the field; and afterwards build thine house.
Proverbs 24:27

Learn by Watching and Listening

Keep your eyes open. As you travel, watch for those who are good workers. As you pass houses, observe to determine the character of those within who are the caretakers of the house. Look for finished work that you would like to copy, and watch for workers who are sincerely seeking to please their employers with their work.

Listen more than you speak. Listen while your employer is correcting or teaching other employees. Listen carefully when he is speaking to you. Watch him carefully as he demonstrates how to do a job. Find out exactly how you should do the job in order to please the one you work for.

I WENT BY THE FIELD OF THE SLOTHFUL,
and by the vineyard of the man void of
understanding; And, lo, it was all grown over with
thorns, and nettles had covered the face thereof,
and the stone wall thereof was broken down.
THEN I SAW, AND CONSIDERED IT WELL; I
LOOKED UPON IT, AND RECEIVED INSTRUCTION.
Proverbs 24:30-32

THE PASSING OF THE HORSE
NO FURTHER USE FOR HIM.
SEE OUR STAND AT THE SHOW.

"What Job Should I Seek?"

If you are seeking the Lord's will, there will be no question about the job that you take. He will clearly guide you to a job that will help you as well as allowing you to be a help to others. If you sincerely seek His will, then you will have peace when making a final decision. Col. 3:15

Never make a decision about a job based on the amount of money that you might earn. Prov. 28:20 Money, convenience, and availability may be considered – but not to be sought above the Lord's will. His will for you may provide you with a good supply of money, but it is just as likely that His will will be rich in experience rather than rich in money. Especially while you are young, consider experience of greater value than money. Never consider a job, no matter how wonderful the benefits, if you would be required to work on Sundays, to listen to rock music all day, to sell alcohol, or to compromise Biblical standards in some other way. Heb. 10:25 Jer. 10:2 When a job causes you to violate Scriptural convictions, then you can be sure that it is not God's will, but rather a temptation to go in the wrong direction.

When seeking the Lord's will, you must surrender your own will. The job that He gives you may not be the kind of work that you would be interested in, but it will be that which He knows you will need as part of your training for future service for Him.

Wherefore be
ye not unwise,
but understanding
what the will of
the Lord is.
Ephesians 5:17

First Job Application

When applying for most jobs, you will be required to fill out an application. Job history is of great importance to your new employer. He will likely want to call your former employer to find out what kind of worker you were, how faithful you were, and how well you got along with others. Having no formal job history, think about how you would answer the questions below. 1 Sam. 17:32-37

Karat & Dial Clock and Watchmakers
Application For Employment

1) Describe your attitude when asked to do messy, difficult jobs around your house.
2) Describe your work habits. Are you a careful, hard worker?
3) List those things that you have learned to do that might be useful in your work.
4) What is your attitude toward those who will spend their day telling you what to do?
5) Describe your use of time in jobs that you have done.
6) Describe your attitude when asked to do a hard job that you don't know how to do.
7) How do you get along with people who are unkind to you?
8) References – List two people (other than immediate family) that we can contact who could tell us about your work habits, your attitude, your dependability, and your obedience.

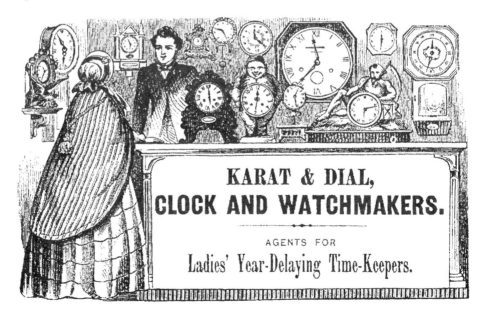

KARAT & DIAL,
CLOCK AND WATCHMAKERS.

AGENTS FOR
Ladies' Year-Delaying Time-Keepers.

"How Would You Like to Have this Done?"

As you should daily seek the Lord's will in all that you do, you should also seek the will of your employer. If you are not sure about the details of the job, be willing to ask. Some employers will want a better quality job that takes more time; others are more concerned about the time spent, and may desire to sacrifice in quality. One employer just wants the grass cut, while another wants his yard to look like a golf course. Be willing to adjust the quality of your work and the time that you spend doing the job according to the instructions that you receive.

After you have been assigned a job by a new employer, be willing to seek clear instruction. Show your willingness to be submissive to his desires, and ask questions so that you can do the job exactly as he wants it done. Your way of doing the job may be right, but the one who has hired you is paying you to have it done his way.

Exhort servants to be obedient unto their own masters, and to please them well in all things; not answering again. Titus 2:9

53

"I Can Do All Things"
Philippians 4:13

When you seek the Lord's will for a job, He will provide you with the necessary ability to complete the assignment that you are given. Phil. 2:13 You may be assigned to do things that you have never done before. Instead of saying, "I can't do that," or "I don't like to do that," be eager to learn. "I have never washed windows before, but if you will show me how to do it, I will do my best." A job is a wonderful opportunity to learn to do new types of work or to operate different kinds of machines – skills that you are likely to need later in life.

Whatsoever thy hand findeth to do, do it with thy might; for there is no work, nor device, nor knowledge, nor wisdom, In the grave, whither thou goest. Ecclesiastes 9:10

Don't Waste Time!

An employer will pay you for your services during a certain time period. He has the right to expect you to follow his directions for what you will do during the time that you are required to work. To the employer, time is money. If you waste time, you waste his money. If you work too slowly, then you are taking more of his money than you deserve. If you stop working to talk (to another employee or to someone on the phone), you are using your employer's money to please yourself.

Many wasted moments turn into hours over a period of time. A lack of enthusiasm for your work can cause you to waste these moments. A habit of watching the clock, hoping for the end of your work time, will likely cause you to be discouraged in your work. Time will seem to go faster when you keep your mind on your work and seldom watch the clock.

Walk in wisdom toward them that
are without, redeeming the time.
Colossians 4:5

"Endure Hardness"

Thou therefore endure hardness, as a good soldier of Jesus Christ. 2 Timothy 2:3 In any work that you do, be willing to patiently and pleasantly bear physical or mental discomfort. Learn to endure a day of demanding work while you are hot, tired, or sore. Learn to tolerate, with a pleasant attitude, boring, repetitious work. It is likely that you are being paid to do something that someone else either cannot do or does not want to do.

As a Christian, all of your work should be done *as unto the Lord.* Col. 3:23 Thinking about all that He has done for you and has promised to you throughout all of eternity, it is not difficult to tolerate, with a quiet peace and joy, any difficult work that you may be asked to perform. It is through difficulties that He will continue to make you stronger in character and, therefore, more useful to Him. Job 23:10 Rom. 5:3,4

Knowing that of the Lord ye shall receive
the reward of the inheritance; for ye serve
the Lord Christ. Colossians 3:24

"Am I Doing This Right?"

With a sincere attitude, seek critical evaluation of your work. The best worker is one who can be corrected and instructed – and then is willing to change according to the desires of his master. A wise employer can watch the way that you work and then teach you how to be a more efficient worker. An eager learner who seeks to improve will grow in favor with his employer. Luke 2:52

You may have had much training and experience, but there are always others who can help you to become more efficient in your work. "Is this the way that you want this done?" "Let me know if there is any way that I can be a better worker." You may have washed hundreds of windows, but be willing to listen to each new employer as he explains how to wash windows at his house or business. Do not seek praise, but do seek to become the best worker that you can be. John 7:18

I delight to do thy will, O my God: yea,
thy law is within my heart. Psalms 40:8

The Froward Master

Sometimes the Lord will give you a job where you will be under the command of an unpleasant employer. You may be treated unfairly, criticized because of your faith in Jesus Christ, and given the worst jobs. In all of this, never assert your "rights" as a worker, but continue to be submissive to authority, seeking to go out of your way to be an obedient and loyal employee.

Suffering wrongfully for the cause of Jesus Christ is acceptable to God. 1 Peter 2:19,20 This is to be the difference between a Christian and those in the world. The unsaved person rises up in rebellion when treated improperly, seeking to defend himself. The Christian depends upon the Lord for deliverance, and until that deliverance comes, is faithful to God in his work. Rom. 12:14,16-19 Prov. 24:29

Servants, be subject to your masters with
all fear; not only to the good and gentle,
but also to the froward. 1 Peter 2:18

"I Will Be Back in Six Hours"

Having left you a list of jobs to do, your employer leaves for the rest of the day. Your work while not being watched should be work that pleases the Lord. *And whatsoever ye do, do it heartily, as to the Lord, and not unto men.* Col. 3:23

Do your jobs thoroughly in the order in which you are expected to do them. Your employer should be able to trust you to work alone because you have *endured, as seeing him who is invisible.* Heb. 11:27 Prov. 15:3

While your employer is absent, you have many unspoken responsibilities. Stay alert as you work, and be aware of what is going on around you. Whereas before you had someone to turn to in time of trouble, now you may be required to make more serious decisions if something goes wrong. Gen. 39:4 Be ready to answer the phone, to meet someone at the door, or to take on other responsibilities as necessary. Prov. 25:19

WHO THEN IS A FAITHFUL AND WISE SERVANT,
whom his lord hath made ruler over his household,
to give them meat in due season? BLESSED IS THAT
SERVANT, WHOM HIS LORD WHEN HE COMETH
SHALL FIND SO DOING. Matthew 24:45,46

Keep Yourself Fit

Keep your body healthy and active. Eat a balanced diet without a lot of "junk" foods and sugar. Get some physical exercise every day, and get enough sleep so that you can be an alert and attentive worker. Most of all, for your health, keep yourself right before the Lord. This is the best source of physical health. Prov. 3:5-8 Prov. 4:20-22 1 Tim. 4:8

Be willing to prepare yourself mentally. If you are given a job that requires more knowledge than you now have, study on your own to learn more about how to do the job. If you are given written material to study, diligently work to learn all that you are expected to know. Learn proper terms so that you can discuss your work with your employer in an intelligent manner. Ask questions and seek to learn more about your work from others. If possible, practice your work at home to become more proficient.

A merry heart doeth good like a medicine: but
a broken spirit drieth the bones. Proverbs 17:22

"Tell Him That I'm Not Here!"

A "requirement" of some jobs may be that you are expected to tell outright lies or to "bend the truth" for your employer. You may even be asked to steal, to change figures, or to do something else that you know is wrong to do. If you have to choose between losing your job or being dishonest, your only choice is to politely explain why you were not able to cooperate – as you leave your job. Never seek to grow in favor with your employer by compromising Biblical standards. Jer. 2:33

Other employees may be offended if you are a more ambitious worker than they are. They may expect you to work in a way that makes their poor work look acceptable – because "everybody" works in such a manner. The Bible says that you should work *not as menpleasers; but in singleness of heart, fearing God*. Col. 3:22b

Then Peter and the other apostles
answered and said, we ought to obey
God rather than men. Acts 5:29

The Other Employees

Most of the time there will be others working for the same employer that you work for. As a Christian, it is up to you to keep the atmosphere peaceful and work-oriented. 1 Thes. 4:12 Unless it is a part of your job, avoid socializing while you work. Talking takes your mind and your eyes off of your work and sets a poor example for others. 1 Cor. 9:27

Other employees will sometimes attempt to irritate you, especially when they find out that you are a Christian. You must purpose in your heart to be steadfast and unmoveable in maintaining a pleasant attitude. Prov. 15:1 Dan. 1:8 1 Cor. 15:58 It is only in this way that you can be a witness for the Lord while you work. *Follow peace with all men, and holiness, without which no man shall see the Lord.* Hebrews 12:14

And that ye study to be quiet, and to do your
own business, and to work with your own hands,
as we commanded you. 1 Thessalonians 4:11

The Tools of the Trade

On many jobs, you will be entrusted with expensive and possibly dangerous tools. Observe all safety precautions, and be mentally alert while you work. Care for tools as if you were responsible for buying them. Be sure to run machinery or handle tools in the proper manner. Through your work, let your employer know that you are not careless or impulsive in your work with his tools or machines.

If a tool or machine breaks while you are using it, be sure to report this to your employer. Be willing to make minor repairs as you work with tools. When you finish using a tool, machine, or appliance, try to put it away in better condition than when you started using it. Clean the grass off of the lawnmower, scrape the soil off of the shovel, or scour out the sink.

In some situations, if you can do better work with your own tools, you may be allowed to bring them to your job. Be sure that your employer knows about this so that he does not suspect you of taking his tools when you leave. 1 Thes. 5:22 If you must use tools that are not proper for the job, do the best work you can with a pleasant attitude.

But as one was felling a beam, the axe head
fell into the water: and he cried, and said, Alas,
master! for it was borrowed. 2 kings 6:5

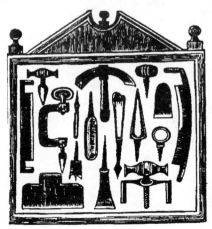

"A Good Name"
Proverbs 22:1

And David gat him a name when he returned from smiting of the Syrians in the valley of salt, being eighteen thousand men. 2 Samuel 8:13 Of course, King David had a name before he went out to battle, but when he returned, he had earned a more descriptive name – given to him by the people. He was building his reputation as a leader. First, just King David; now King David, *THE GREAT MILITARY LEADER*.

In like manner, whenever your completed work is inspected by your employer, you will "gat a name" as a worker that is more descriptive than your given name. Instead of Sarah, you will become Sarah, *a good worker*, or Sarah, *a waster of time*. Be an enthusiastic, joyful worker; not impulsive and careless. Work in such a way that your employer never has any opportunity to question your value as an employee. Be dependable and trustworthy. When away from your job, remember that what people think of you reflects upon the person that you work for. If you seek to build your reputation through honest, hard work, you will never have trouble getting a job.

A good name is rather to be chosen than great riches, and loving favour rather than silver and gold. Proverbs 22:1

"Ye Are My Witnesses"
Isaiah 43:10

Always be a witness for Jesus Christ through your obedience, cooperative attitude, and gracious speech. You should be so different from unsaved workers that your employer should take notice and be glad of this difference. Your Christian life should show through your promptness, your honesty, and your hard work. Jesus Christ should also be seen through the pleasant expressions on your face. Prov. 27:19 Neh. 2:2

When you have the opportunity, be ready to be a witness through your spoken word. Unless you have permission, do not do this on your employer's time, but take advantage of lunch periods, breaks, and free time before and after work. Carry a small New Testament or a selection of tracts to use if you are given the opportunity. Prov. 11:30

But sanctify the Lord God in your hearts: and
be ready always to give an answer to every man
that asketh you a reason of the hope that is
in you with meekness and fear. 1 Peter 3:15

Finish the Job!

Leave no job unfinished. Do all that you are expected to do, and then make sure that the mess is cleaned up, the tools are put away, the machines are turned off, and the doors are closed. Some jobs may take several days or weeks to complete, but at the end of your work each day you can put all things in order. 1 Cor. 14:40

Even before you complete the first job that you have been assigned, you may be given a second or third job to be completed immediately. When you have spare time, try to complete the first job that you were given. An employer should be able to trust you and should not have to check to see that each job is completed. Be willing to stay late or to arrive early in order to accomplish what you have been given to do. Complete your work in such a way so that your employer could say, *"Well done, thou good and faithful servant."* Matthew 25:21

Jesus saith unto them, my meat is to do the will of him that sent me, and to finish his work. John 4:34

Receiving the Rewards

The rewards of work are many and include money, experience, strengthened character, personal satisfaction (having helped others), and human praise. Let none of these cause you *to think* [of yourself] *more highly than* [you] *ought to think; but to think soberly, according as God hath dealt to every man the measure of faith.* Romans 12:3b Having done what you may consider to be an excellent job, always have the attitude of *we are unprofitable servants: we have done that which was our duty to do.* Luke 17:10b   Having pleased your employer, remember to *let another man praise thee, and not thine own mouth; a stranger, and not thine own lips.* Proverbs 27:2

You may become well-known as a good worker, but always keep in mind that as strong and able as you may get, the Lord *delighteth not in the strength of the horse: he taketh not pleasure in the legs of a man. The LORD taketh pleasure in them that fear him, in those that hope in his mercy.* Psalms 147:10,11 Any glory is due to Him, as we simply perform our reasonable service. *But he that glorieth, let him glory in the Lord.* 2 Corinthians 10:17

For who maketh thee to differ from another? And what hast thou that thou didst not receive? Now if thou didst receive it, why dost thou glory, as if thou hadst not received it? 1 Corinthians 4:7

Handling the Money

Always be thankful for that which you are paid in exchange for your work. Be content with what the Lord has provided for you. Phil. 4:11 Have no desire to become rich, as *they that will be rich fall into temptation and a snare, and into many foolish and hurtful lusts, which drown men in destruction and perdition.* 1 Timothy 6:9 *He that hasteth to be rich hath an evil eye, and considereth not that poverty shall come upon him.* Proverbs 28:22

All that you receive comes from the Lord, and all should be used according to His will. 1 Cor. 4:2 First, be sure to give back to Him in tithe and offering to the local church. Mal. 3:10 1 Cor. 16:12 Always be willing to help others with money that the Lord has allowed you to have. Ep. 4:28 Acts 4:32:32-35 There is no need to hoard money or to use it all to provide unnecessary luxuries for yourself. Those who freely give according to the Lord's direction will never suffer lack. Luke 6:38

Let him that stole steal no more: but rather let him
labour, working with his hands the thing which is
good, that he may have to give to him that needeth.
Ephesians 4:28

Advancement

The unsaved person, as he gets older, expects to have promotions and higher pay. God's "promotions" for you as His child are always what you need – not necessarily another job or position that would give you more authority and more pay. True advancement is to follow the Lord's direction in life, even if He directs you to a new type of work with less pay. Prov. 3:5 *Thou wilt shew me the path of life: in thy presence is fulness of joy; at thy right hand there are pleasures for evermore.* Ps. 16:11

Accept the Lord's method of moving you to a new job. You may no longer be needed, you may be fired, or you may be let go because of a false accusation. Having to leave a job due to a false accusation can help to direct you to your next job (a good worker may have too many options). Rom. 8:28

Do not seek to become a boss. James 3:1 Ps. 75:6,7 The most important job that you can get, although a job that may have little pay or honor, is the job that the Lord desires for you to have. Always have the attitude of, *Lord, what wilt thou have me to do?* Acts 9:6 Luke 16:10

For a day in
thy courts is
better than
a thousand.
I had rather be
a doorkeeper in
the house of my
God, than to
dwell in the tents
of wickedness.
Psalm 84:10

Keep Looking Ahead

Many look ahead and prepare for retirement. A Christian must look ahead and prepare for eternity. As you work where the Lord places you, you are preparing for your eternal work. Mt. 25:14-30 Is. 64:8 Do not be concerned about having houses, lands, a good retirement program, or the luxuries of this life. Mt. 19:29 Ps. 37:25 Seek to do all that you can for the Lord and not for yourself. Mt. 16:24 Never turn back to the attractions of this world by chasing after a high-paying job. Heb. 11:15,16 Forget the "easy," high-paying job and the honors that you may have had in the past, and *press toward the mark for the prize of the high calling of God in Christ Jesus.* Phil. 3:13,14

And Jesus said unto him, no man, having
put his hand to the plough, and looking back,
is fit for the kingdom of God. Luke 9:62

POLITE MOMENTS

Chapter 4

How to Be a Servant

"I Must Be about My Father's Business"
Luke 2:49

When He was twelve years old, Jesus had one interest above all others – to be a servant to His heavenly Father. In John 5:30 Jesus said, *"I seek not mine own will, but the will of the Father which hath sent me."* The Lord's business for you is to learn to be a submissive, faithful servant. You must practice this every day with your parents, so that when you become an adult, you will know how to be a willing servant for the Lord Jesus Christ.

A servant is one who voluntarily yields himself to the commands of the one who is his master. A servant is willing to give up what he wants to do in order to do what his master wants him to do. To be a servant of God is a great privilege and of great importance to God. *He that is greatest among you shall be your servant.* Mt. 23:11

All Christians, children and adults, are to be servants – this is the purpose of the Christian life. Your parents serve you in obedience to the Lord, Who commands them to *train up a child in the way he should go.* Prov. 22:6 Although parents are servants, God places them over you as your masters, whom you must obey! Ep. 6:2

And the Lord said unto the servant, Go out into the highways and hedges, and compel them to come in, that my house may be filled.
Luke 14:23

"It Is Not in Man That Walketh to Direct His Steps"
Jeremiah 10:23

God did not give you the ability to make your own decisions and to direct your own daily life. You must learn that to have a successful life you must be obedient to those whom the Lord places in authority over you. When you whine, argue, complain, or fail to obey, you are *trying* to direct your own life. God's way is for you (and for your parents) to **obey them that have the rule over you, and submit yourselves.** Heb. 13:17a God's way is for you to recognize (acknowledge) the authority above you and to allow them to direct you in your daily life. **Commit thy way unto the LORD; trust also in him; and he shall bring it to pass.** Ps. 37:5

Unless you are given a free choice in the matter, you should eat what you are given to eat, do what you are told to do, go where you are told to go, and refrain from doing that which you are told not to do.

And he said to them all, If any man will come after me, let him deny himself, and take up his cross daily, and follow me.
Luke 9:23

"Speak, for thy servant heareth."
1 Samuel 3:10

"He Hath Served
With Me in the Gospel"
Philippians 2:22

John, writing about Timothy, said *"ye know the proof of him."* Timothy had proven himself to be a willing servant– *as a son with the father.* Timothy had been a loyal, faithful servant to Paul. A son (or daughter) serving with his or her parents should present an excellent example of a master-servant relationship.

You have an important part in your family's service for the Lord. All of your attention, desire, and energy should be given to fulfil this important position. *My son, give me thine heart, and let thine eyes observe my ways.* Prov. 23:26 You should not live in a "separate world" with your own plans, but you should "give your heart" to your parents. To them you are to be loyal, obedient, and willing to follow in whatever direction they guide you. As your parents serve the Lord, you are to serve under them, in submission, and with them, in the work God has called them to do. The family works together as one unit and for one purpose – the daily will of Jesus Christ for the family.

Then answered Jesus and said unto them, Verily, verily, I say unto you, The Son can do nothing of himself, but what he seeth the Father do: for what things soever he doeth, these also doeth the Son likewise. John 5:19

"I Do Always Those Things That Please Him"

John 8:29

As a servant, you must always seek to please those who are in authority above you. To please another person, you must do exactly what they would want you to do in the way in which they would want you to do it. You must be alert to know and to do all of those things that they tell you to do. Listen carefully when you are given instruction. If you are uncertain about your parent's will, be sure to ask them. "Is this how you want this to be done?" "Is my attitude what you would like it to be?

A servant also tries to know unspoken desires of his master. Your parents cannot tell you everything for every situation. Whenever you have to make decisions about what you should do or how you should do something, your first thought should be, "How would my parents want me to do this?" "Would doing this please my parents?" "What would my parents tell me to do if they were here with me?" As you get older, you should then ask yourself, "What would the Lord want me to do in this situation?" *With my whole heart have I sought thee: O let me not wander from thy commandments*. Ps. 119:10 *And ye shall seek me, and find me, when ye shall search for me with all your heart.* Jer. 29:13

Take fast hold of instruction; let her not go: keep her; for she is thy life. Proverbs 4:13

76

"When He Hath Tried Me"
Job 23:10

Learning to become a faithful servant is not always easy. You will have to fight against the desires of your flesh and *flee youthful lusts.* You also need to receive correction and discipline. *We have had fathers of our flesh who corrected us, and we gave them reverence.* Heb. 12:9a Your parents will help to train you to become a better servant, and you should be thankful for their time, concern, and effort on your behalf. *Behold, happy is the man whom God correcteth: therefore despise not thou the chastening of the Almighty.* Job 5:17

Many times things will not happen the way you want them to– but as a servant, you must learn that *in whatsoever state I am, therewith to be content.* Phil. 4:11 Those who allow the work of God and of their parents in their lives are the ones who will *come forth as gold.* Job 23:10 *For it is God who worketh in you both to will and to do of his good pleasure.* Phil. 2:13 It is the love of the Lord and the love of your parents that causes them to correct you, to discipline you, and to prove you through difficult circumstances. *For whom the Lord loveth he chasteneth, and scourgeth every son whom he receiveth.* Heb. 12:6 *He that spareth his rod hateth his son: but he that loveth him chasteneth him betimes.* Prov. 13:24

Obey them that have the rule over you, and submit yourselves: for they watch for your souls, as they that must give account, that they may do it with joy, and not with grief: for that is unprofitable for you.
Hebrews 13:17

"Here Am I; Send Me"
Isaiah 6:8

At all times, a servant must make himself available to follow his master's next desire. When the call comes, immediately stop what you are doing and respond to the call. A servant does not have his own plans in life; he is always on the alert to follow the will of his master. When God needed someone for a job, Isaiah answered right away. He did not wait to see if someone else would step forward to follow God's plan. The apostle Paul said, *"Lord, what wilt thou have me to do*?" Acts 9:6 David said, *"Is there not a cause?"* 1 Sam. 17:29

Be attentive to what your parents say. Be alert to what needs to be done around the house. It is unwise to compare your service with someone else's. To say "It's not my turn to help," or "I helped last time" shows an unwilling attitude. Remember that it is a special honor to be a servant of the Lord. Rather than trying to get out of things to do, try to find more ways to be of service. Be willing to serve without expecting something in return, such as pay or honor, and without expecting the job to be easy. *And let us not be weary in well doing: for in due season we shall reap, if we faint not.* Gal. 6:9

For we dare not make ourselves of the number, or compare ourselves with some that commend themselves: but they measuring themselves by themselves, and comparing themselves among themselves, are not wise.
2 Corinthians 10:12

"I Will Never Leave Thee, Nor Forsake Thee"

Hebrews 13:5

A servant has the position of being cared for by a master. As a servant, you have no need to worry. Security is the condition of being content and safe. A servant trusts in his master to provide for all of his needs. A servant trusts in his master to plan his daily activities. *In all thy ways acknowledge him, and he shall direct thy paths.* Prov. 3:6 As a servant later in life, you can securely trust in the Lord for your marriage plans, your work in life, a place to live, a car to drive, etc. In all areas of life a servant yields himself to the master, who in turn guides, protects, provides, and *is a friend that sticketh closer than a brother.* Prov. 18:24

A servant does not seek his own will and can trust in the Lord (your parents while you are young) to help him to do those things that seem to be too hard. Instead of the constant frustration of chasing after his own lusts, one who has chosen to serve seeks only one thing– to know and to do the desires of his master. *That he no longer should live the rest of his time in the flesh to the lusts of men, but to the will of God.* 1 Peter 4:2 *Let your conversation be without covetousness; and be content with such things as ye have: for he hath said, I will never leave thee, nor forsake thee.* Heb. 13:5 While it is a joy to be a servant, one who chooses to live selfishly will have a difficult life! *Good understanding giveth favour: but the way of transgressors is hard.* Prov. 13:15 Deut. 28:1,2,14,15

Thou wilt show me the path of life: in thy presence is fulness of joy; at thy right hand are pleasures for evermore.
Psalm 16:11

"As Seeing Him Who Is Invisible"
Hebrews 11:27

Moses endured (kept on doing what the Lord wanted him to do) as if he could see God, Who is invisible. *The eyes of the LORD are in every place, beholding the evil and the good.* Prov. 15:3 *Thou understandest my thought afar off.* Ps. 139:2 God knows your every thought. God sees everything that you do. Even when you are alone or with friends, you should serve your parents *as if* you could see them watching you.

A servant must serve his master, not just his master's eyes. Many change their behavior because the eyes of authority are not watching them. *Servants, obey in all things your masters according to the flesh; not with eyeservice, as menpleasers; but in singleness of heart, fearing God ... for ye serve the Lord Christ.* Col. 3:23,24

Whom having not seen, ye love; in whom, though now ye see him not, yet believing, ye rejoice with joy unspeakable and full of glory.
1 Peter 1:8

"I Delight to Do Thy Will"
Psalm 40:8

Is it your delight to be of service? Is serving something that you eagerly look forward to? Does it make you joyful to do what your parents have asked you to do? Since your purpose for being alive is to be a willing servant to the plans of your Saviour, then while you are young you must also learn to be this kind of a servant. Your parents, who have done much for you since you were born, should be given your joyful service. The Lord Jesus Christ, Who has shed His blood to pay the penalty for your sins, has shown much greater reason for you to serve Him with gladness. 1 Cor. 6:19,20

One who delights to serve does not frown, sigh, groan, or otherwise show that he is displeased with what he is asked to do. You should delight to serve because of your love for the one whom you are serving– not because of the kind of job that you are given. *Serve the LORD with gladness.* Ps. 100:2 Daniel, having been captured and taken from his family to a strange land, still had an *excellent spirit.* Dan. 5:12

We are
the servants
of the God
of heaven
and earth.
Ezra 5:11

"By Love Serve One Another"

Galatians 5:13

Being set free from being a slave to the devil, God now asks us to become servants of one another. No longer being forced to sin, we now must choose to live for the Lord or to live according to the desires of our old nature. *Use not liberty for an occasion to the flesh.* Gal. 5:13a *Yea, all of you be subject one to another, and be clothed with humility.* 1 Peter 5:5

How can you become a servant to other Christians? There are many areas in which we can be a help to others. There are simple things like picking things up, helping with jobs, and offering to help when you see a need. Other areas where you can help are in encouraging others, comforting others, protecting others, and praying for others.   In doing these things you become a servant of other people. Remember that your body and your possessions belong to the Lord and are to be used to be of service to others. 1 Cor. 10:24 Rather than trying to promote yourself, *Let no man seek his own, but every man another's wealth.* We must follow our Lord and Savior, Jesus Christ, who *made himself of no reputation, and took upon him the form of a servant.* Phil. 2:7a

By this we perceive the love of God, because he laid down his life for us: and we ought to lay down our lives for the brethren.
1 John 3:16

"Do All to the Glory of God"

1 Corinthians 10:31

You should serve the Lord in such a way that your service brings honor to Him. Others watching you will then see that you are different because you desire to give up your own way so that you can please the Lord.

Often when children misbehave, the parents are blamed. Your parents receive either honor or shame as a result of your attitude, speech, and behavior. *A wise son maketh a glad father: but a foolish son is the heaviness of his mother.* The foolish, self-willed son or daughter brings sorrow to his parents. The wise son or daughter brings joy. It is a joy to parents when their children do that which is right at home and in public. 3 Jn. 4 Children then bring honor to their parents.   You must try to be the kind of servant to the Lord (Rev. 4:11) and to your parents so that you will never cause them to have a bad name because of your speech or actions. *But I had pity for mine holy name, which the house of Israel had profaned among the heathen, whither they went.* Ez. 36:21

The father of the righteous shall greatly
rejoice: and he that begetteth a wise child
shall have joy of him. Proverbs 23:24

"Hello there, Young Lady!
What would you like to
do when you grow up?"

"Well, fine Sir, that's all
settled. I shall become
a servant of the Lord!"

"The Affairs of This Life"
2 Timothy 2:4

A faithful servant has one focus in life – that of pleasing his master. He does not get involved in anything else that causes him to get his eyes off of his one purpose in life. He does not become entangled *with the affairs of this life*.

Keep your thoughts on that which is important in life– being a faithful servant. *And truly, if they had been mindful of that country from which they came, they might have had opportunity to return.* Heb. 11:15 Although you may live in a country where any material pleasure may be bought, as a Christian you are a servant of the Master of another country– Heaven. Things that you "treasure" on earth will get in the way of your faithful service to Him. Mt. 6:19-21 Keep your interests set on *things above.* Col. 3:1,2 *He that loveth father or mother more than me is not worthy of me. He that findeth his life shall lose it: and he that loseth his life for my sake shall find it.* Mt 10:37a; 10:39

The most important thing that you can learn as a young person is how to be a servant! Those who do not choose to be servants will become a friend of the world, and *whosoever therefore will be a friend of the world is the enemy of God.* James 4:4 Demas, once a servant, forsook Paul, *having loved this present world.* 2 Tim. 4:10 *Love not the world, neither the things that are in the world.* 1 Jn. 2:15a

No man can serve two masters: for either he will hate the one, and love the other; or else he will hold to the one, and despise the other. Ye cannot serve God and mammon. Matthew 6:24

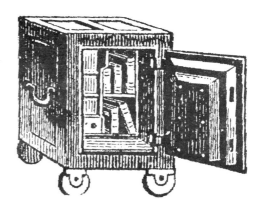

"Without Me Ye Can Do Nothing"

John 15:5b

A servant must never develop a self-assured, know-it-all attitude. *For if a man think himself to be something, when he is nothing, he deceiveth himself.* Gal. 6:3 *And if any man think that he knoweth any thing, he knoweth nothing yet as he ought to know.* 1 Cor. 8:2 Jesus Christ, God in the flesh, lived fully dependent upon his Father. *I can of mine own self do nothing .... I seek not mine own will, but the will of the Father which hath sent me.* Jn. 5:30

A servant, in order to be faithful, must know the perfect will of his master. It is important to seek advice and counsel often from your parents. Seek counsel for decisions you have to make, for the way that you act, for the way that you do work, and for the attitudes that you show. Seek clear direction in all of these areas; keep no secrets from your parents, and be willing to discuss the most personal of matters, including problems, future plans, and needs. *The way of a fool is right in his own eyes: but he that hearkeneth unto counsel is wise. Hear counsel, and receive instruction, that thou mayest be wise in thy latter end. Every purpose is established by counsel: and with good advice make war.* Prov. 12:15; 19:20; 20:18 The young person who talks often with his parents is likely to become an adult who finds conversation with the Lord in prayer to be natural and necessary. *When thou saidst, Seek ye my face; my heart said unto thee, Thy face, LORD, will I seek.* Ps. 27:8

I will instruct thee and teach thee in the way which thou shalt go: I will guide thee with mine eye. Psalm 32:8

"I Keep Under My Body"

1 Corinthians 9:27

The old nature that is within each Christian desires to have its own way, to be in control, and to lust after *the pleasures of sin.* Heb. 11:25 These desires to be in charge of your own life and to fulfil your lusts must not be followed! *Likewise reckon ye also yourselves to be dead indeed to sin, but alive to God through Jesus Christ our Lord.* Rom. 6:11

At all times, you should learn to refuse your own desires when these desires go against Biblical commands or instructions that you have received. *But I keep under my body, and bring it into subjection. 1* Cor. 9:27a Knowing that *in me (that is, in my flesh,) dwelleth no good thing*, you need to be fully obedient to your parents and to the Lord – refusing to do that which you feel like doing. Rom. 7:18   Prov. 12:15

Neither yield ye your members as instruments of unrighteousness to sin: but yield yourselves to God, as those that are alive from the dead, and your members as instruments of righteousness to God.
Romans 6:13

"Yet Have I Made Myself Servant Unto All"

1 Corinthians 9:19

Although free from all men, Paul made himself a servant unto those he met who were unsaved. He was willing to be a help to them, and then was willing to serve them by explaining God's plan of Salvation.

To show your willingness to serve, be ready to help others with acts of kindness. Seek your parents' advice first, and then help another person without seeking gain for yourself. *To the weak became I as weak, that I might gain the weak: I am made all things to all men, that I might by all means save some.* 1 Cor. 9:22 To the elderly, unsaved lady next door, I "am made" into a volunteer leaf raker so that I can get a chance to tell her about Jesus Christ. To the cashier at the store, I "am made" into a person who is thankful for her help so that I can get an opportunity to give her a Gospel tract. A person who has been provided with a helpful service is much more likely to listen to what you have to say.

Even as the Son of man came not to be ministered unto, but to minister, and to give his life a ransom for many. Matthew 10:28

87

"Do it with Thy Might"
Ecclesiastes 9:10

Do with the best of your ability *whatsoever thy hand findeth to do.... for there is no work, nor device, nor knowledge, nor wisdom, in the grave, whither thou goest.* A servant must be *zealous of good works.* Titus 2:14   A servant should excel in all that he does. A servant should not quit or do a poor job because he is not good at something or because he does not like to do something. It is the difficult jobs that will build your character the most. Doing things that are hard for you will help you to learn to become a better servant.   *Thou therefore endure hardness, as a good soldier of Jesus Christ.* 2 Tim. 2:3

While you are young, you must work hard to prepare to be a diligent servant of the Lord Jesus Christ. *It is good for a man that he bear the yoke in his youth.*   Lam. 3:27 To be fit for His service, you must learn to be an enthusiastic servant– so that when you become an adult, you will be *meet for the Masters use.* 2 Tim. 2:21

Prepare thy work without, and make it fit
for thyself in the field; and afterwards
build thine house. Proverbs 24:27

"Delight Thyself Also in the Lord"

Psalm 37:4

When you take great pleasure in your parents, it is not difficult to know what they expect from you, and it becomes your greatest desire and delight to please them by being obedient to them. When you delight in the Lord, He will lead you by giving to you the desires that you are to have. It is the desires of the heart that guide one in all the activities of life. Our own desires are selfish desires. Jer. 17:9 A servant must not have selfish desires, but must diligently seek to delight himself in his master and in his master's will so that he will know how to live his daily life. *And I will delight myself in thy commandments, which I have loved.* Ps. 119:47 *Neither have I gone back from the commandment of his lips; I have esteemed the words of his mouth more than my necessary food.* Job 23:12

A servant who delights in his master is one who will be freely honored with blessings that the master is able to bestow. A faithful servant can expect to receive all the promises of his master for protection, provision, and help. *He will fulfil the desire of them that fear him: he also will hear their cry, and will save them.* Ps. 145:19 *If ye abide in me, and my words abide in you, ye shall ask what ye will, and it shall be done unto you.* Jn. 15:7

One thing have I desired of the LORD, that will I
seek after; that I may dwell in the house of the LORD
all the days of my life, to behold the beauty of the
LORD, and to enquire in his temple. Psalm 27:4

"What Things Were Gain to Me"

Philippians 3:7

...*Those I counted loss for Christ.* A servant seeks no gain for himself, but seeks to promote his master. A loyal servant does not seek to be noticed, but by his work draws attention to his master. The man who was sent to seek a wife for Isaac desired to be known only as *Abraham's servant.* Gen. 24:34 John the Baptist, when asked who he was, simply referred to himself as *the voice.* Jn. 1:23 About Jesus Christ, he said, *"He it is, who coming after me is preferred before me, whose shoe's latchet I am not worthy to unloose. He must increase, but I must decrease."* Jn. 1:27; 3:30

A servant's "promotion" should be given only by his master, and this promotion gives the servant the privilege of more areas of service with more responsibility. An unfaithful, lazy servant brings attention to himself, and is a discredit to his master. *Confidence in an unfaithful man in time of trouble is like a broken tooth, and a foot out of joint.* Prov. 25:19 *The slothful man saith, There is a lion in the way; a lion is in the streets.* Prov. 26:13

So likewise ye,
when ye shall have
done all those things
which are commanded
you, say, We are
unprofitable servants:
we have done that which
was our duty to do.
Luke 17:10

"Daniel Purposed in His Heart"
Daniel 1:8

Daniel was a faithful servant of the Lord because he had made a firm decision *not to defile himself.* A servant must remain clean in mind and body. *But as he who hath called you is holy, so be ye holy in all manner of conversation.* 1 Peter 1:15 Carefully guard you mind from the things of this world shown on T.V. or on the internet. *I will set no wicked thing before my eyes.* Ps. 101:3 Keep your thoughts pure (2 Cor. 10:5, Phil. 4:8) and keep your body pure. *That everyone of you should know how to possess* [keep] *his vessel* [body] *in sanctification and honor.* 1 Thes. 4:4

To keep pure you must refuse to listen to what this world has to teach you. *Cease, my son, to hear the instruction that causeth to err from the words of knowledge.* Prov. 19:27 *Thus saith the LORD, Learn not the way of the heathen.* Jer. 10:2 As a dirty dish is not useful for the next meal, so an unclean (with sin) boy or girl is not useful in the Lord's service. *I would have you wise unto that which is good, and simple concerning evil.* Rom. 16:19b

Keep thy heart
with all diligence;
for out of it are
the issues of life.
Proverbs 4:23

"It Is Required in Stewards"

1 Corinthians 4:2

A steward is one who is to care for something that is of value; a steward must be found faithful. A servant is a steward, with no rights or possessions of his own. Even his own body belongs to his master. 1 Cor. 6:19,20 *What hast thou that thou didst not receive? now if thou didst receive it, why dost thou glory, as if thou hadst not received it?* 1 Cor. 4:7 A servant is also a steward of God's truth to be delivered to others. *But as we were allowed by God to be put in trust with the gospel, even so we speak; not as pleasing men, but God, who trieth our hearts.* 1 Thes. 2:4 You are a steward of all money and things that the Lord allows you to have. Things are for your use in this life as you serve the Lord, but– *they that buy, as though they possessed not; And they that use this world, as not abusing it: for the fashion of this world passeth away.* 1 Cor. 7:30,31 *The things which are seen are temporal; but the things which are not seen are eternal.* 2 Cor. 4:18b

Take care of things and money, using them only according to the will of God, and always be willing to freely give to others who are in need – according to the will of God. A steward must be busy *distributing to the necessity of saints; given to hospitality.* Rom. 12:13 Remember, *it is more blessed to give than to receive.* Acts 20:35b

And the multitude of them that believed were of one heart and of one soul: neither said any of them that any of the things which he possessed was his own; but they had all things common.
Acts 4:32

"Choosing Rather To Suffer Affliction"

Hebrews 11:25

God's servants will sometimes be called upon to suffer affliction as a part of their service. *For to you it is given in the behalf of Christ, not only to believe on him, but also to suffer for his sake.* Phil. 1:29 Whatever happens, a servant must be *faithful unto death*! Rev. 2:10

It is a servant's love for his master that enables him to suffer for his sake. The more you love your parents, the more willing you will be to do any difficult thing that they ask you to do. Gen. 37:1-14 *There is no fear in love*– one who loves his master is willing to go anywhere, to do anything, and to rejoice in the suffering that may come. 1 Jn. 4:18 Paul and Silas, having been beaten with *many stripes upon them*, cast into prison, and put into stocks, *prayed, and sang praises to God.* Acts 16:25 The apostles, beaten and commanded to not speak in the name of Jesus Christ, *departed from the presence of the council, rejoicing that they were counted worthy to suffer shame for his name.* Ac 5:41

Beloved, think it not strange concerning the fiery trial which is to try you, as though some strange thing happened to you: But rejoice, seeing ye are partakers of Christ's sufferings; that, when his glory shall be revealed, ye may be glad also with exceeding joy.
1 Peter 4:12,13

"Well Done, Thou Good And Faithful Servant"

Matthew 25:21

What wonderful words to hear! Someday, *every one of us shall give account of himself to God*. Rom. 14:12 Your service for the Lord on this earth begins when you are saved. You will account for how you have lived your Christian life – how willing you were, as a servant, to follow the will of the Lord for each day of your life. *I press toward the mark for the prize of the high calling of God in Christ Jesus.* Phil. 3:14

To be asked to follow the Lord means that He has a definite plan for your life. If you are willing to follow this plan, He will make it clear to you. *My sheep hear my voice, and I know them, and they follow me.* Jn. 10:27 As a servant of the Lord you must not follow the advice or commands of satan as he daily tempts you to go against God's will for your life. *And a stranger will they not follow, but will flee from him: for they know not the voice of strangers.* Jn. 10:5

If any man serve me, let him follow me; and where I am, there shall also my servant be: if any man serve me, him will my Father honour. John 12:26

94

LEARN TO DO THESE THINGS!

Chapter 5

Learn to
Work Quietly

Think of others as you do your work. Work quietly so that they can think about their own work without having to listen to you and think about your work!

Study to be quiet.
1 Thessalonians 4:11a

Learn to
Sit Still

When you sit still, you can listen better and learn better. Wiggling takes thought away from what you should be thinking about. Keeping your hands in constant motion by turning every pen or pencil into a rocket ship will keep you from knowing WHAT YOU OUGHT TO KNOW! *Be still and KNOW...*

Be still, and know that I am God.
Psalm 46:10a

Learn to
Listen

To learn you must first learn to listen. To listen you must stop talking and think about what another person is saying. *My son, attend unto my wisdom, and bow thine ear to my understanding.* Prov. 5:1 One who does not listen carefully will not have understanding!

Therefore, my beloved
brethren, let every man be swift
to hear, slow to speak.
James 1:19a

Learn to
Memorize

Of what use is school when what you are taught goes "in one ear and out the other?" Learn to carefully think about what you hear or read so that you memorize it for future use. Think about what you have learned at a later time, and be determined to keep it in your memory.

Take fast hold of instruction; let her not go: keep her; for she is thy life.
Proverbs 4:13

Learn to
Think of Others

Look not every man on his own things, but every man also on the things of others. Phil. 2:4 Consider the needs of others and always be ready to help and to encourage others!

**Let nothing be done through
strife or vainglory; but in lowliness
of mind let each esteem other
better than themselves.**
Philippians 2:3

Learn to
Be Content

You have the best home, the best teachers, the best family, and the best body that you could have – because they are the ones given to you by the Lord. Be thankful for what you have, and do not be envious of those who seem to have things better than you do. *Let your conversation be without covetousness; and be content with such things as ye have: for he hath said, I will never leave thee, nor forsake thee.* Heb. 13:5

Better is the sight of the eyes than the wandering of the desire: this is also vanity and vexation of spirit.

Ecclesiastes 6:9

Learn to
Be Pleasant

Instead of frowning, being bossy, irritable, or grouchy, be easy to get along with and a joy and a help to others. Give to others a joyful personality!

If it be possible, as much as lieth in you, live peaceably with all men.
Romans 12:18

Learn to
Have Initiative

A person with initiative does not need to have the teacher by his side every minute. He listens, knows what to do, and does whatever he can without help. He is a "self-starter," and works hard to do whatever he is asked to do.

I press toward the mark for the prize of the high calling of God in Christ Jesus.
Philippians 3:14

Learn to
Think Before
You Speak

Instead of blurting out what first comes to mind, think about what you are going to say first. Then decide if what you will say is the right thing to say!

Set a watch, O LORD, before my mouth; keep the door of my lips.
Psalm 141:3

Learn to
Control Your Thoughts

While other things are going on around you, learn to keep you mind on what you are to be doing. When you think about your work, you won't be daydreaming, playing with something, or watching others.

Casting down imaginations, and every high thing that exalteth itself against the knowledge of God, and bringing into captivity every thought to the obedience of Christ.

2 Corinthians 10:5

Learn to
Be Patient

Learn to quietly wait to talk to your teacher, wait for other children, and to wait for things that you want. *Be patient toward all men.* 1 Thes. 5:14b   Be patient when things are hard for you, *knowing this, that the trying of your faith worketh patience.* James 1:3 *Wait on the LORD: be of good courage, and he shall strengthen thine heart: wait, I say, on the LORD.* Ps. 27:14

Better is the end of a thing than the beginning thereof: and the patient in spirit is better than the proud in spirit.
Ecclesiastes 7:8

Learn to
Serve the Lord With Gladness

Psalm 100:2a

Why art thou cast down, O my soul? and why art thou disquieted within me? hope in God: for I shall yet praise him, who is the health of my countenance, and my God. Wherefore lift up the hands which hang down, and the feeble knees. Ps. 43:5 Heb. 12:2

You have the special joy of serving your Creator – the Creator of the universe and of all living things. Let nothing else make you more happy than to be His willing servant in all that you are asked to do!

Learn to Be
Neat & Orderly

Keep your papers neat and clean and your books orderly. Know where your pencils and pens are, and be able to quickly find important papers. If you are neat and orderly you will not have to say, "I can't find it," or "I lost it." Your work area should always be pleasing to your teacher!

Let all things be done decently and in order.
1 Corinthians 14:40

Learn to
Work Hard

I went by the field of the slothful, and by the vineyard of the man void of understanding; And, lo, it was all grown over with thorns, and nettles had covered the face thereof, and the stone wall thereof was broken down.

Proverbs 24:30,31

Whatsoever thy hand findeth to do, do it with thy might; for there is no work, nor device, nor knowledge, nor wisdom, in the grave, whither thou goest.

Ecclesiastes 9:10

It is good for a man that he bear the yoke in his youth.

Lamentations 3:27

110

Learn to
Follow

To follow means that you are obedient to all that you are told to do. You follow the one who is leading you to do something that will be helpful to you or something that will be helpful to another person. A disobedient person thinks that they know what is best to do, but the Bible says *the way of man is not in himself: it is not in man that walketh to direct his steps.* Jer. 10:23 *Obey them that have the rule over you*! Heb. 13:17

My sheep hear my voice, and I know them, and they follow me.
John 10:27

Learn to
Deny Yourself

Many things that you will be asked to do will not be fun, easy, and what you want to do. To deny yourself means that you always are ready and willing to do whatever you are asked to do by those who are placed over you by God.

And he said to them all, If any man will come after me, let him deny himself, and take up his cross daily, and follow me.
Luke 9:23

Learn to
Receive
Correction

Your parents and teachers are commanded to *withhold not correction from the child.* Prov. 23:13a *A child left to himself bringeth his mother to shame.* Prov. 29:15 Be thankful when you receive correction! Ask for forgiveness and start doing what you are asked to do!

Reproofs of instruction
are the way of life.
Proverbs 6:23b

Learn to
Mind Your Own Business

And that ye study to be quiet, and to do your own business, and to work with your own hands, as we commanded you.

1 Thessalonians 4:11

Learn to

Control Your Emotions

Must you shriek when an ant crawls across the floor, moan when you can't figure out a problem right away, and whine when you get thirsty? Must you erupt in anger, dismay, frustration, or surprise when you could calmly face each situation that comes along?

He that hath no rule over his own spirit is like a city that is broken down, and without walls.
Proverbs 25:28

Learn to
Fear the Lord

The fear of the LORD is the beginning of knowledge: but fools despise wisdom and instruction. Prov. 1:7 The person who learns the most is the one who has a fear of doing that which is wrong. This is a fear that you should have!

Come, ye children, hearken unto me: I will teach you the fear of the LORD.
Psalm 34:11

Learn to
Do Well

Isaiah 1:17a

Always work so that your parents and teachers could say of you, "Well done, thou good and faithful child!" (From Mt. 25:21) Do well so that you can have a good name. When you name is mentioned before other people, what do they think of you? Somebody is watching you, so ALWAYS DO WELL!

A good name is rather to be chosen than great riches, and loving favour rather than silver and gold.

Proverbs 22:1

Other Titles From Plain Path Publishers

Christian Character
For Boys and Girls Ages 10-14

Christian Manhood
For Boys Ages 11-14

Christian Leadership
For Boys and Girls Ages 11-16

Rooted In Christ
A Foundational Discipleship Study

What Saith the Scripture?
Training the Next Generation At Home

Plain Path Publishers
P.O. Box 830
Columbus, NC 28722

www.plainpath.org